LOUISE D. JEWELL

Midnight Musings for the Adult in Me

A Memoir – Book Two

Dedicated
to all those
who have ever felt
- different -

Sam saw a white star twinkle for a while. The beauty of it smote his heart, as he looked up out of the forsaken land, and hope returned to him.

— J.R.R. TOLKIEN, LORD OF THE RINGS

Contents

A Word from the Author

Dear Reader,

I believe that no adult should ever stop asking questions. The kind of questions that inspire you to think about the things you think about. And feel about.

This book is a collection of answers to questions I have been asked over the years. And in these responses, I weave my own life story.

Some stories are lighthearted. And others take on a more serious tone.

One of my favourite hobbies is being lost in thought. And despite the strange looks that came my way when I was a child, I never stopped wondering.

- About Life.
- About Death.
- And everything in between.

My best time for reflection is when most folks are fast asleep. Hence, the meaning behind the title, *Midnight Musings for the Adult in Me*.

As you read through these midnight musings, may you be encouraged to explore the questions in your life journey. No matter how challenging, complicated or even comical the themes may be.

With love and respect,
Louise

Musing #1: A Dream Come True

"Blessed is the man who has found his work, let him ask no other blessing." — Robert Louis Stevenson

A Dream Come True

Twenty years ago, I had a dream.

I was standing on the road in front of our home. The trunk of the car was opened. In the trunk lay a thick manuscript wrapped in brown paper and held together with twine.

I whispered, "God, is it time?"

He gently replied, "No. Not yet."

It wasn't yet time to pen my story. This is because I had more journeying to do. And that was fine by me.

Twenty years later.

How time flies. Here I am, composing my second memoir, *Midnight Musings for the Adult in Me*.

You asked, "Do you dream?"

Yes, I dream. A lot.

And in this case, you might call it a dream come true.

Musing #2: On Pins and Needles

꩜

"For a highly sensitive person, a drizzle feels like a monsoon."
— Anonymous

On Pins and Needles

Not long after dreaming of the unpublished manuscript, I experienced yet another dream.

This time, I was sitting in the driver's seat. A string, like a clothesline, was attached to the driver's side mirror outside the windshield.

This clothesline extended off into the horizon. Blankets, towels, and clothes were pinned onto the clothesline, obstructing my view.

What in the world?

Why is this clothesline here?

I can't see a thing!

7

Upon waking, I pondered the dream and its message. The following impressions came to mind.

I couldn't see to drive because I had "heaps of laundry" to take care of. These items (clothes) represented issues I still needed to deal with. One at a time. Like you do when you've washed your clothes. You hang up the clean items one at a time.

The dream was particularly significant because, as a child, Mom had numerous clotheslines strung up on the side of the house. She didn't have a dryer.

I also had a clothesline that could hold three loads of laundry at my place. I loved using it even though I had a dryer.

Then, I dreamt of a clothesline.

Since the clothesline was integral to my life, I included it in a rug I created. This section is part of a larger rug I called "Seasons," as in the seasons of my life.

If you look closely, you will see a royal blue-and-gold dress hanging on the far right of the clothesline. This represents the same dress I wore the night I won my first public-speaking trophy. The dress also had three gold buttons, but one popped off. But I didn't care as I didn't worry about fashion.

So much fussing the night before.

"Mom! Do I have to wear these curlers to bed?"

One look from Mom told me it was best not to argue. And so I slept with what felt like pin cushions jammed up against my head. Not fun.

And then there was the anxiety of forgetting my lines for my speech. Fortunately for me, the judges would be very forgiving. Because I did blank out. And they gave me a second chance.

As I could not get a ride, I ended up spending the night in the home of my competitor. Her house smelled incredible. And her Mom, Mrs. Earle, was wondrously hospitable.

Mrs. Earle declared, "Time to change, girls!"

For the public-speaking event, my faithful Mom had sent me to school with my dress-up clothes, ready to go.

How do I put these on?

I was mortified at the sight of the hideous garter belt and equally ridiculous nylons. Give me a pair of coveralls; I would have been as happy as a clam.

The dress felt scratchy, and the stockings sagged at the knees. How miserable I felt. My curls were immaculate, thanks to the stinky hairspray Mom had used. To this day, I prefer to wear 100 percent cotton. Forget about curls. And stockings? Those went bye-bye the year I entered premature menopause.

Usually, I rode on a school bus that took close to an hour. But this time, I got to ride in Mrs. Earle's car. A lovely ride it was, too; it took less than ten minutes. No motion sickness for me on that ride!

Upon arrival at the school, students came racing toward us.

"Congratulations, Louise! You won the trophy!"

Overwhelmed. Ecstatic. Grieved.

Overwhelmed with all the attention, probably due to being a highly sensitive person (HSP), which I describe in a few pages at the end. Ecstatic that I had won first prize. Grieved that I had defeated my kind competitor.

I had difficulty processing this massive bundle of emotions. Not surprising for an eleven-year-old.

At lunchtime, I discovered Mrs. Earle had filled my lunch box with yummy food. As a result, my tummy never growled the whole day.

And that is the story behind the royal blue-and-gold dress. And the dream that inspired me to recall this story. A time when I was overwhelmed with delight and despair.

All at the same time.

Musing #3: Meat and Potatoes

"You can only come to the morning through the shadows."
— J. R. R. Tolkien

Meat and Potatoes

At what age did reality hit you?

It was a typical Saturday afternoon, and the skiing conditions were perfect. However, on that particular day, I chose to stay indoors and searched for a quiet place to be alone.

To think.

"What does a twelve-year-old think about? And what would keep a kid indoors on a beautiful sunny day of all-day skiing?

I lived right smack beside a ski hill. So when Dad built our house, he decided to buy a lot right next to the slopes. As Mountain Manager, Dad liked the short commute.

Dad's job had one big perk, complimentary ski passes for each family member. Meaning my six siblings and me, including Mom and Dad. We all skied for free. No charge for day and night tickets. You might say it was a win/win for everyone.

Yep, we lived really close to the ski hill.

I noticed my two ski buddies waving their arms, "Lou, get out here and join us!"

But I had other things on my mind. And I needed to talk it out with someone.

Someone I respected.

Preferably an adult.

That's when Mom entered the room.

I looked up from my journal and exclaimed, "Mom, why am I here? What does my life all mean?"

Mom shook her head and attempted a smile, "Louise, you know we love you. You think too much. Look, it's a beautiful day. Go out and ski with your friends."

I swallowed hard and wiped away my tears.

Who could help me now?

You asked, "What is reality?"

I see now how I was questioning reality and my existence. I wanted to know,

- Do I matter?
- What is truth?
- What's real?
- What do I believe?

And that was the day I decided to keep asking questions and searching for meaning.

It was a long road.

And I was up for it.

Musing #4: Thinking Outside the Box

"A creative man is motivated by the desire to achieve, not by the desire to beat others." — Ayn Rand

Thinking Outside the Box

How did you study? Did you use any special tricks to help you remember the material?

I wish I could show you my study cartoons from college.

Did you say, "Study cartoons"?

16

Yep.

I sketched cartoons in college as a way to memorize facts.

You see, I learn best by seeing, not by hearing.

And as a learning tool, I drew silly cartoons.

My study cartoons represented entire essays. Pages of information were captured in minute detail.

I once drew cartoons during the first thirty minutes of a two-hour exam. And using those drawings as my template, I aced it.

By using this skill, I brought down my anxiety.

How so?

Each fanciful cartoon portrayed pages and pages of facts. And so, that is how I overcame exam anxiety.

Reflection:

I just realized why this method of studying was both fun and effective. I was engaging my right brain as well as my left brain. Very cool. There's nothing like using your whole brain in the learning process.

Musing #5: No More Secrets

"The worst loneliness is to not be comfortable with yourself."
— *Mark Twain*

No More Secrets

I was twelve years old and had held a dark secret for almost two years.

My body was changing, and I didn't like it. In fact, I was terrified. I believed I was ugly. And even hideous.

One day, I knew I could hold my secret no longer.

"Mom, I'm a monster!"

Mom stopped peeling potatoes. "Louise, why would you say that?"

And that was the first time I revealed my secret. That my body was changing. Had been changing for months.

I wiped my tears with a tea towel.

"Oh, Louise. Every girl's body changes as she grows up. And your body is no different. You are normal."

Was Mom telling me the truth?

"How about this? I will take you to the doctor who will tell you the same thing. How's that idea?"

Clever Mom.

Two weeks later, Mom smiled as we walked out of the doctor's office. "There! See? Now, do you believe me?"

I sighed with relief.

And that was the day I accepted the truth. That I was not a monster. Not ugly.

Just an average girl.

Going through puberty.

You might wonder, "Am I pretty? How can I learn to accept myself?"

The first step to believing I was an attractive person was to accept my body and let it become my friend. It was not an overnight success story. It took me many years to become friends with my body.

Many years.

Musing #6: A Short Fuse

"A soft answer turns away wrath, But a harsh word stirs up anger."
— Proverbs 15:1 NKJV

A Short Fuse

Have you struggled with anger?

Once upon a time, I had a short fuse.

And a sharp tongue.

That mouth got me into trouble. More than once.

One day, I snapped at a colleague. Just because I was grumpy.

Later that night, I tossed and turned with guilt. I also felt deep shame.

It was time to change my ways.

Right then and there, I resolved to do things differently.

I decided to observe wise people. What they said. How they spoke. And when they stayed silent.

And this is what I discovered.

Wise people:

1. uphold their word
2. learn from the past
3. keep their cool
4. know how to say no
5. possess a moral code
6. own up when they blow it
7. make no time for gossip
8. welcome honest feedback

Musing #7: When Push Comes to Shove

"The fear of man brings a snare, But whoever trusts in the Lord shall be safe." — Proverbs 29:25 NKJV

When Push Comes to Shove

In some ways, I was a late bloomer.

I didn't get my driver's license until I was twenty-eight.

When I first learned how to drive, I was taught to check the mirrors. One day, I was so focused on what was in the rear view mirror, I nearly hit a car in front of me.

Note to self: Lou, keep your eyes on the road!

Likewise, if I am forever looking over my shoulder, caring too much about what others think, I will get myself into trouble.

26

So what should I do?

- I need to concentrate on where I'm headed.

What should I not do?

- I'd best not focus on what others are thinking and saying. About me.

You asked, "Why do we care so much about what other people think? What's the term for that?"

The Bible calls it *the fear of man.*

When I fear what other people think of me, I am left paralyzed. Stuck.

And that is no way to travel in life.

What is the secret that helped me stop worrying about the opinion of others?

I learned to fear God instead.

And what *He* thinks of me is really all that matters.

Musing #8: Breathing Space

"Ah! There is nothing like staying at home, for real comfort."
— Jane Austen, Emma

Breathing Space

What does that say about your social life if you enjoy spending time alone?

When I started writing full-time, a friend asked, "Aren't you lonely?"

Lonely?

No. Not when I am at peace doing what I feel called to do.

Once upon a time, I believed I had to accept every social invitation. And if I wanted to leave a party early, I worried I was being rude.

In my effort to please others, I grew more and more exhausted.

29

And depressed.

It got so bad that I cringed whenever an invite came my way.

And then, one day, I realized that it was all right to like my own company.

That's when my way of thinking changed.

I discovered:

- It's acceptable to say, "No, thank you."
- My craving for alone time is a legitimate need.
- It's okay if I leave a party early.
- I can want a rich social life and need solitude. The two can co-exist.

So, now when I consider an invitation, I ask myself four questions:

1. First, do I have the energy (interpersonal or physical) for this?
2. Second, do I have time on my calendar?
3. Third, do I need to do this?
4. Fourth, do I want to do this?

In fact, I am asking myself these very same questions today. And already, there is no way I can say yes to every request this week.

Just no way.

And that's perfectly okay.

Musing #9: All That and a Bag of Chips

❦

"From there to here, from here to there, funny things are everywhere!" — *Dr. Seuss*, One Fish Two Fish Red Fish Blue Fish

All That and a Bag of Chips

Have you ever met a person and immediately knew they were awful?

I was a fifty-four-year-old divorcée when I decided to enter the dating world. What better way than to attend my first Meetup group?

The theme was "Red Flags in Dating."

I located the meeting room and poked my head in the doorway.

Louise, it's just a workshop. You can do this.

Twenty-three people filled the room. Nine of them were men.

The facilitator, a dating coach, threw out this question: "What kind of behaviour do you see needs to happen in dating?"

Responses came fast and furious:

- Date a while before you decide on "the one."
- Consult with your friends. Get their opinion.
- Don't stop living your life.
- Sex on the first date. Guaranteed!

Oh, my, the dating scene is not much different today than it was thirty-five years ago.

(Silly me) I raised my hand and offered the following:

"A healthy relationship needs trust, transparency, communication, work, and play. And as for sex, well, that would be way down the line."

What I thought was, *And sex for me only would happen in marriage. Period.*

More discussion followed.

The workshop wrapped up.

The dating coach invited us to stay and mingle.

Moments later, one of the men approached me.

He pointed his finger straight at me and bellowed, "Lady, I can tell you are new to dating. If a man doesn't get sex by the third date, he will not hang around. I mean, get real! When you're over fifty, time's short, and what man has time to wait around for a woman to have sex? So take my advice and change your thinking. I have interviewed all the men here tonight, and they all say the same thing."

I smiled. "Thank you for your take on this. Clearly, you speak from your worldview, and I appreciate that."

"Yeah. Well. Good luck!" And with that, he spun around and stormed out the door.

A woman on my right quipped, "Wow, he sure has strong opinions."

I smiled again, shook my head, and didn't say a single word.

Musing #10: Falling into Place

"Not until we are lost . . . do we begin to find ourselves."
— *Henry David Thoreau,* Walden

Falling into Place

What is the most memorable thing that anyone has ever said to you?

We had just moved to a new city, and I was homesick. My friends lived 2,402 kilometres away. The only people I knew in town were my beloved mom and dad-in-law.

I was anxious. My husband's new job never materialized upon our arrival.

I was nervous. We were living on savings, and the pot was almost dry.

I was alarmed. How would we buy food when our emergency fund was depleted?

I was desperate. The vacancy rate was almost nil. The only place we could find to rent was a dingy basement suite with rats in the walls and slugs on the kitchen floor.

I was heartbroken. I had left a rewarding career with great pay. My dream to be a stay-at-home mom had vanished. I now had to go back to work. Again.

Yes, I was feeling many emotions. I was also feeling guilty about feeling those negative emotions.

Our new pastor and his wife invited us to lunch one Sunday after church. Talking with them was easy, and I found their manner soothing. I was sipping my tea when the unthinkable happened.

I burst into tears.

And that's when our host, Arnie Toews, said something I will never forget. "Your feelings are not wrong, Louise. It's what you do with them that counts."

- That one sentence validated my feelings.
- That one sentence helped me identify my feelings.
- That one sentence motivated me to get professional help.
- That one sentence inspired me to find my voice.

And now you know another reason I used to say: It's never too late. Never.

Musing #11: Learning Curve

"A child of five would understand this. Send someone to fetch a child of five." — Groucho Marx

Learning Curve

Do you try to learn new things? How often?

I usually learn a new skill when I have no choice but to do so.

Like when I had to say goodbye to my flip phone and upgrade to a flat phone (aka Android smartphone). Weeks went by, and I kept missing incoming calls.

Tap, tap, tap went my finger on the screen. The call dropped and went straight to voice mail.

I fumed, "What is wrong with this phone?"

39

Finally, I just gave up.

"Why can't they make phones like they used to?"

It was time to get some coaching.

So I googled the phrase, "How do I answer a call on an Android phone?"

The online tutor demonstrated how to "swipe" my phone. Just so you know, when I was a kid, swipe meant the same as "steal."

How times change!

When I misplaced my cell phone, a family member offered to call it. Several rings later, I located my flat phone in the laundry basket.

When I was a kid, we never lost our phone. That's because the family telephone sat in the hallway. On a shelf. And there it remained with the cord firmly attached to the wall.

Musing #12: How Time Flies

⚜

"When I write, I can shake off all my cares." — *Anne Frank,* The Diary of a Young Girl

How Time Flies

What are you passionate about?

You know you are passionate about something when time just flies.

And you never even noticed it was dark outside (Like now. I just looked out the window, and it is already pitch black. When did that happen?)

Or when your stomach starts to growl, and you realize you never ate dinner. And it's already nine o'clock at night.

This happens to me. A lot.

What passions fire me up and motivate me to be my very best?

When I write, I feel at home. And like Eric Liddell once said in the movie *Chariots of Fire*, "I feel God's pleasure."

Liddell ran like the wind.

I write and never get winded.

Okay, a few other passions. Well, let's see.

- Before I retired as a clinical counsellor, I enjoyed working with motivated clients. They reminded me of how courageous people can be.
- As a friend, I treasure our heart-to-heart talks. Some of our conversations can last up to five hours. And that's even on the phone. So just imagine how long our chats would last if we enjoyed tea together.
- I can spend hours drawing cartoons without a care in the world.

Time truly flies when you're doing what you really love.

Musing #13: Kicking Up a Fuss

"In general my children refuse to eat anything that hasn't danced in television." — Erma Bombeck

Kicking Up a Fuss

Sometimes, kids compare you as a parent to other parents. How should a parent handle that, especially if it hurts your feelings?

- Why can't we have cable like everybody else?
- Why do I have to do chores when my friends don't?
- You're the strictest mom in the whole school!
- Why can't we have a flat-screen TV like so-and-so?
- Her mom let her get a nose ring. Why can't I have one too?

Did it hurt when my children talked to me like that?

Sometimes, yes.

But all the time, I knew this: I was the adult in this relationship.

My kids were just that. Kids.

They had yet to learn I was doing my best with the limited resources we had.

My children have now grown up.

- One owns a flat-screen TV.
- The other prefers a laptop.
- And neither chooses to wear a nose ring.

Motherhood.

I wouldn't trade it for the world!

Musing #14: Sick at Heart

"There is no harm in being afraid. The only harm is in doing what Fear tells you. Fear is not your master! Laugh in his face and he will run away." — *George MacDonald,* Lilith

Sick at Heart

When I discovered my first serious boyfriend had betrayed me, I felt like dying.

I was seventeen. What did I know about love?

What I did know was that my heart was broken.

Over time, I found life too much to cope with. So I began to sleep with men. Men I had only just met.

But the pain never went away.

For seven long years, I struggled with bulimia in another effort to cope. I searched for places to purge. Yet deep within, the void remained, no matter how much food I stuffed down.

Many years later, I finally came to the end of myself. I thought, I can't live like this anymore.

I was too scared to say the word. Depression.

Depression?

I'd say more like despair. I was in a very dark place.

I get why people take themselves out.

I get why they commit suicide.

It's not that they don't want to live anymore.

They just want the pain to stop.

I thank God I reached out for help even though it took me years. But finally, I made that first appointment to see a therapist.

Yes. I get what it means to want to end my life.

And from those hard life lessons, I learned this: Nothing was wasted.

So what's different about my life now?

- I no longer isolate.
- I no longer live in shame.
- I no longer pretend.

I surround myself with real friends who, like me, know how to be vulnerable.

Transparent.

Real.

And together, we encourage each other to be who we were always meant to be.

Ourselves.

Musing #15: The Angel of Death

"All the world's a stage." — *William Shakespeare,* As You Like It

The Angel of Death

How do actors not fall in love when they have to kiss each other in movies?

I used to wonder the same thing. That is until it was my turn, and I experienced my first kissing scene on stage with a young man.

We'll call him Bob.

Bob was a popular student in our high school drama class. I, on the other hand, was a shy student. And you might say Clumsy was my middle name.

Our drama teacher chose me to play the part of an elderly and senile grandma who sits in a sandbox the whole time. And she is visited by the Angel of Death, who kisses her on the forehead. Not what you would call a romantic scene.

And yes, the play was called *The Sandbox*.

Can you imagine rehearsing the same kissing scene ten times? With several cameras pointed in your face? Add to that all the bright lighting. (That *really* drove me nuts.)

But then, what do I know about professional theatre on stage or in films? My only acting experience was in high school.

So what was my most exciting moment on stage?

It was the day the Angel of Death kissed me right smack dab on . . . the forehead. While I sat in a sandbox, playing the part of a grandma.

A grandma who had lost her mind.

My first and only stage kiss.

In grade 10.

What an amusing memory.

Musing #16: The Birds and the Bees

"What do girls do who haven't any mothers to help them through their troubles?"
— Louisa May Alcott, Little Women

The Birds and the Bees

Mom called out from the living room, "Louise, come in here. I'm talking to your big sister about the birds and the bees. You can listen too."

I stopped dead in my tracks.

And broke out in a cold sweat.

"No way! I'm not listening to that yucky stuff."

And with that, out the door, I fled. My mother's reprimand trailed behind me. "Louise! Don't be so stubborn."

The last thing on my mind was the birds and the bees. I was ten years old and just wanted to be a kid. And at that moment, all I could think of was to climb my favourite tree, curl up with my Nancy Drew Mystery Stories, and read.

In peace.

Fast forward two years.

To my horror, I discovered blood on my underwear one summer afternoon. "Mom! I'm bleeding to death!"

Mom rushed into the bathroom, took one look, and grinned. "Louise! You're a woman now!" Life as I knew it crashed before my eyes.

"No, Mom! I don't like this."

Ever the practical mom, she answered, "Well, you can't stop it, Louise. Now listen to me. You're going to bleed every month from now on."

"Every month?"

"And you need to be careful. You can now have babies."

Did Mom just say, "Babies"? I had three younger siblings and vaguely remembered them as babies at one time or another. But I, myself, had no interest in babies. Never mind having one myself.

"But Mom, I just want to climb my tree! How can I do that when I'm bleeding all over the place?"

Mom pursed her lips and shook her head. "You need to stop climbing trees, Louise. And start acting like a lady."

She then pulled out a sanitary napkin from below the sink. "Here, put this belt on and attach the ends like this." I looked at the hideous white belt and knew we would never be friends.

Following this tedious (and necessary) tutorial, I flew down the hill toward my climbing tree. Then, with a heavy heart, I hugged it one last time. "Goodbye, my friend."

Fifty years later.

What I once considered a nuisance was really a gift. To bear children. And to now have the joy of being called Gramma Lou.

Musing #17: Dressed to the Nines

"Don't cry because it's over. Smile because it happened."
— Ludwig Jacobowski

Dressed to the Nines

What were the 1970s like for teenagers?

Platform shoes were all the rage in the mid-seventies. My big sister looked so stylish in her new shoes. So I decided to buy myself a pair too.

That's when I discovered I was terrified of heights. A few days later, I wore my new shoes to school. We rode the bus back and forth to school. One day, my shoes and I had a bit of a disagreement. Coming down the bus steps, I tripped and catapulted into the ditch next to the road.

Oops! Time to throw away those shoes! I never wore them again.

In those days, you never dreamed of holding a private telephone conversation. Unless you were in a telephone booth. I can still hear Dad yelling from the kitchen, "Get off the phone! Did you hear me?"

He only had to tell us once.

We lived in a ski resort surrounded by farm country. So if you didn't live in my town, you were a long-distance call away. I never dared call long distance from home.

Bell bottoms were hip, and so were pilot frames. I jumped up and down when Mom let me choose wire-rim eyeglasses. The following weekend, I went for a snowmobile ride as a passenger. We hit one bump, and the driver slammed backwards into my face.

Snap! went my eyeglasses frames. Money was tight. And poor Mom was not happy. So my ugly old cat-eye glasses came to the rescue. Gag.

I welcomed my very first bicycle when I was fourteen. It was a second-hand ten-speed. A gift from my best friend. More than one gear on a bike was a big deal in those days.

I heard Bob Dylan for the first time when I was fifteen. And I was never the same after that. I also listened to Aretha Franklin, Creedence Clearwater Revival, and Smokey Robinson.

Who can forget that classic, "I Heard It through the Grapevine"? I loved that song and played it again and again until I memorized the lines, dancing to the beat as I sang.

Mom adored music too.

Some days, she'd stop what she was doing and invite us to dance with her in the living room. She never had to ask twice.

We were not permitted to wear blue jeans at school. Any student caught wearing denim received a detention slip. One day, the whole student body got fed up and formed a protest. We marched around the school, chanting in unison.

It's surprising what a thousand high school students can do to change the system. Not long afterwards, word came down the pipe. Fridays were now called Jean Day.

We had been heard.

I was in grade 9 when I blew my first bubble. By accident. In science class. Big mistake. Chewing gum was forbidden in school. I don't recall that rule ever changing.

Mom enjoyed a particular brand of tea. The kind that came with a trinket tucked inside the box. I noticed those same trinkets sitting on a shelf in an antique shop. They went for a pretty penny.

One morning, I discovered a drinking glass stuffed inside a bag of wheat puffs.

Can you picture getting away with selling something like that today? It's a wonder we didn't find shards of glass in our cereal bowl.

Mom decided it was time to switch to a new laundry detergent. All because of the free gift promised inside.

"Louise, look what I found!"

Mom grinned ear-to-ear as she pulled a rolled-up tea towel out from the box. She was like a kid in a candy store.

I hear everything goes now when it comes to fashion, be it bell bottoms or platform shoes. Speaking of which, I wear eyeglasses to this day.

Want to know which pair I fancy the most? My cat-eye glasses, of course.

Some things never change.

Musing #18: Off the Beaten Track

❦

"When the whole world is running towards a cliff, he who is running in the opposite direction appears to have lost his mind."
— Anonymous

Off the Beaten Track

Were you cool as a kid?

I wasn't part of the "in crowd," if that's what you mean.

I grew up in a ski resort. And it was the thing to update your ski equipment and accessories at least once a year. Except I had no interest in doing that.

A family member asked, "You're not going to go out like that, are you?"

How do you explain to someone you will never get bored with your old lace-up ski boots? Especially when they fit like an old, comfortable shoe.

Being in style was never my thing. Comfort was.

And when I did try my hand at being stylish, things went south. Sometimes I even ended up in a ditch.

So I stopped trying to keep up with the latest fashions.

The result?

I felt at ease in my own skin.

So, yeah. I was never cool as a kid.

But here's how I saw it. Even back then, I was cool with not being cool.

Afterthought:

Did you notice the different coloured socks in my illustration above? That's what happens when you dress in the dark for school. Let's just say that was not approved of back in the day.

Musing #19: Going Home

~~~

"Worms, fire, or the sea might consume my body. But my spirit will live in a world with no more wanderings and trials. I do not have to pass through many painful incarnations. Beyond death lies paradise." — *Richard Wurmbrand,* The Oracles of God

Going Home

What hard questions should people ask themselves?

"I'm not sure about cremation, Lou. What do you think?"

"Our wills are out-of-date. Who would you recommend we see?"

My beloved elderly mom and dad-in-law needed support while sorting their end-of-life plans. What better way to help than to get my own house in order?

Like they say in 12-step recovery, "Let it begin with me."

Here are twelve tasks I set out to do (If you find lists boring, just skip down past item #12):

1. Update my will.
2. Secure an executor.
3. Appoint a power of attorney.
4. Make a living will.
5. Buy a burial plot.
6. Choose an urn.

7. Decide on and pay for funeral arrangements upfront.
8. Draft a list of instructions for my executor.
9. Invite loved ones to make a list of any of my possessions they'd love.
10. Gift those belongings now.
11. Pare down the rest of my possessions. And last but not least,
12. Wear a medical bracelet that indicates my wishes in case of an emergency.

Once I got the ball rolling on my end-of-life planning, I was better equipped to help Mom and Dad get their ducks in a row. Sadly, but not unexpectedly, they passed away a short time later.

And you know something?

Planning ahead gave our family true peace of mind. We knew we were fulfilling their last wishes. I hope to do the same for my family when I go home.

So, yeah. I'd say life-and-death questions are good to ask.

Sooner rather than later.

Musing #20: Turn a Deaf Ear

"Blessed is he who has learned to admire but not envy, to follow but not imitate, to praise but not flatter, and to lead but not manipulate." — William Arthur Ward

Turn a Deaf Ear

What should you do if people are jealous of you? And all you're doing is just being yourself?

Sadly, there will always be someone who

- covets what you have
- resents who you are
- talks behind your back and
- envies how you live

And here's the rub. I cannot control what other people think, say, or do. And when I remember that, I'm more at ease. And no longer feel dis-ease.

If I start to stew about such things, I end up in turmoil.

And anyway, who wants to live in other people's heads? Not me.

If my motive is never to inspire jealousy in others, I can sleep at night. In peace.

And that's good enough for me.

Musing #21: All Ears

◦◦◦

"He who has ears to hear, let him hear!" — Matthew 11:15 NKJV

All Ears

What are your weaknesses?

"Louise, are you deaf? Get your nose out of that book and get in here."

"Sorry, Dad! I'll be right there."

When Dad called, you came running. The only problem was that I sometimes did not hear him (or Mom).

To this day, I can tune people out very quickly when I am writing. Or reading. Or just plain thinking. And anyone who doesn't know me well might think I am being rude.

73

I'm not.

I simply don't notice people around me when I am in the zone.

I once went to a hearing specialist to see why my ears were in so much pain. A one-hour hearing test confirmed I have unusually excellent hearing.

We soon figured out the source of the ear pain.

I had recently attended a children's puppet performance. And the sound system was too much for my poor ears. (There's that HSP at work again!)

Some call it selective hearing.

Others might call it the power of concentration.

Musing #22: On Top of the World

"'Listen to the trees talking in their sleep,' she whispered,
as he lifted her to the ground. 'What nice dreams they must
have!'"
— *L.M. Montgomery*, Anne of Green Gables

On Top of the World

Did you ever build a tree house that was your very own?

I was eight years old when I caught sight of the perfect tree. Right below where our new house sat.

I loved that tree. It was easy for me to climb. And it gave me a terrific view of the valley where I lived.

And best of all, my tree house sat at the very top. So if you held on tight enough, you could swing back and forth in the wind. My little brother had a tree fort, too, in the same tree. But his was close to the ground.

I loved to read in my private space. And as I approached my preteen years, I began to brood a lot more. About this world and how I fit into it. Stuff like that. I mostly spent time there in my tree fort alone. But of course, a private hideaway is where it's at when you come from a big family with seven kids.

Back then, I was not allowed to use our one rotary telephone. And forget about sneaking off to make a phone call. Phones in those days were attached to the wall. There was no such thing as privacy when talking on the phone. Especially since it was a party line.

Undeterred, I found a way to contact my two buddies who lived on the other side of the valley.

- One yodel from my tree fort meant, "Hey, wanna come over and play?"
- And two yodels meant, "I'll be right over!"

Living in a valley made yodelling fun. I loved listening to the echoes. When no reply was forthcoming, I went with option two.

I climbed down the tree and ran to their house. They were that close. When you're a child who lives in the country, it helps to have a short commute to your friend's house. That way, you don't need to ask for a ride.

I loved the freedom.

Yep. Those days I could play outdoors to my heart's content, and Mom never worried about where I was. She knew where I hung out.

I was perched in my tree, hiking in the forest, or swimming in the lake.

Or hiding somewhere in the house with a book or my journal.

Oh, and about my tree house. Imagine a plank of wood the size of an old tree swing seat. It was the most straightforward build ever. No nails were needed. I only had to find two fat branches to balance the plank.

Yep. That makeshift tree house was my childhood dream getaway.

Musing #23: Cook Up a Storm

$\sim$ ✦ $\sim$

"I was 32 when I started cooking; up until then, I just ate."
— Julia Child

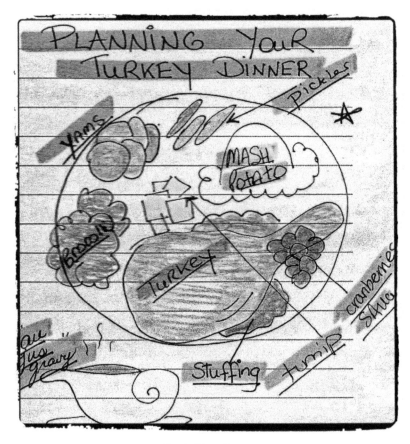

Cook Up a Storm

If you're a cook, what ten rules should you follow?

When I was a new wife at twenty-two, I had no clue how to boil an egg or read a recipe. So my first goal was to learn how to whip up a meal. I poured over a recipe book with a spatula in one hand and a dictionary in the other.

And when I was stuck, I called for help.

My dear mom-in-law came to the rescue.

Pleased to help, Mom walked me through many a recipe.

One day, I baked a pound cake. It was a beautiful golden brown on the outside, and incredible smells wafted through my kitchen.

Success! Or so I thought.

I cut into it. Oops! It was a gooey mess.

"Mom! Why didn't my pound cake bake all the way through? It was raw in the middle!"

She answered me gently. "Did you preheat the oven, Dear?"

"Preheat the oven? What's that mean?"

With the patience of Job, Mom walked me through each step of how to preheat the oven. And finally, "Wait for the light to come on!"

"Oh! So that's what preheating the oven means! Cool!" My next pound cake tasted much better. Whew!

Those were the days before the internet. And folks were used to helping each other out. In real time.

One day, while cooking dinner, a fire started in my oven. Terrified, I called my husband at work. "Come home quickly! The oven is on fire!"

My husband arrived home in time to put out the fire. "It was just some grease that spilled over, Lou. It's okay."

"Wow," I thought, "now I get why cleaning the oven is a bright idea."

After several kitchen mishaps, I decided it was time to change my ways. And so I did what I love to do: I made a list.

Lou's twelve rules (I know you asked for ten!) to live by as a cook:

1. Don't be afraid to ask for help.
2. Honour others by serving healthy foods they enjoy.
3. Cook with a joyful heart.
4. Invite wee ones to draw a picture of what you plan to serve for festive occasions. Little people love to "see" what's on the menu!
5. Remember to preheat the oven.
6. Encourage pleasant conversation at the table.
7. Focus while measuring ingredients. Salt is not sugar, so don't confuse the two.
8. Use a timer. Avoid surprises.
9. Don't scream; try ringing a dinner bell instead.
10. Keep only those cooking tools that work and that you use.
11. Allow others to help with clean-up. And last but not least,
12. When the dog starts licking the oven door, it's time to pull out the oven cleaner.

Musing #24: Nite Nite

"Spiritual maturity is not knowing what to do with your whole life, but just knowing what to do next." — Henri Nouwen

Nite Nite

What advice should you follow every day?

Here's a wise saying I've learned along the way:

> **When you don't know what to do, do the next right thing.**

"But Mom, what if I don't know what the next right thing is?"

My son was a teenager. And he was desperate for an answer right then and there. I took one look at the dark circles under his eyes.

"How about if you call it a night? And then, tomorrow, we can take another look at this question. Does that sound like a good idea?"

He peered out from under the bed covering. "Are you saying, Mom, that the next right thing for me to do is sleep?"

"Yep. You are exhausted. And when we're tapped out, we don't think so clearly."

"Okay, I'll try that idea. Thanks, Mom."

"Tomorrow, it will all be clear. Then, after that, you'll see." And that is what he did. He slept right through the night.

At the breakfast table, my son arrived bright-eyed and bushy-tailed.

"Mom! I think I got it!"

"That's great! Tell me what you came up with!"

I poured another coffee as he popped the bread into the toaster. His eyes gleamed as he laid out his plan.

My son had discovered an important life skill.

When you don't know what to do, do the next right thing.

Even if it is as simple as taking a nap or getting a good night's sleep.

Musing #25: Early Starter

❧

"I'm trying very hard to understand this generation. They have adjusted the timetable for childbearing so that menopause and teaching a sixteen-year-old how to drive a car will occur in the same week." — Erma Bombeck

Early Starter

The year was 1993 when I heard the news.

"Louise, the results came in. It is now confirmed." I pressed the receiver closer to my ear.

"I'm sorry to inform you; you are in menopause."

"Thank you, Lord," I replied.

Why would I say that?

My two pregnancies had been complicated. But I was thankful to be alive and grateful to be a Mom of two beautiful children.

Here I was, a Mom in her early thirties with two children under seven. This was a nonsurgical kind of menopause. The doctor called it premature. Premature is right.

True to my nature, I devoured every book I could find.

I can still see the words now. "Your children have flown the coop. Ask yourself, 'What do I want to do for the rest of my life?'"

I glanced up from the text and examined the LEGO pieces on the floor. One day, my little guy, age five, would be a grown man. And my little girl, age seven, would leave the nest too.

In some ways, I've always been an early starter.

And this time was no different.

I imagined my life fifteen years down the road. Both my children would probably be pursuing undergraduate degrees. That or trekking across Europe.

I reached for paper and pencil and began to make a list. At the top, I wrote,

- What I want to see happen in fifteen years.
- I would like to have earned a graduate degree.
- Well then, what better time to start than right now?

Within the month, I was enrolled in a program that allowed me to work on my master's degree, one course at a time. And best of all, there was no deadline for completion.

Seventeen years flew by.

Where did the time go?

In 2010, I held my certificate of graduation. And wouldn't you know it? The literature I had read years earlier was correct. My children were now prepping for college.

You asked, "How long have you ever taken to complete a goal or a task?"

I would have to say it was working on my master's degree.

Throughout those many years, I raised two children, pursued mental health training, worked outside the home, and provided practical support for my elderly parents-in-law. And all the while, I never put my family in debt.

Do I regret the length of time it took me to complete that task?

No. The learning journey was just how I liked it.

Slow but sure and steady.

Musing #26: Not on Your Life

⸎

"I can't get out of bed, my Fitbit is charging and my steps won't count." — Pugnado @LuvPug

Not on Your Life

You asked, "You probably hold some unpopular opinions. Would you care to name one?"

Just before Mother's Day, my son asked, "Mom, how would you like one of those bracelets that measure how many steps you take?"

"Thank you for asking, son. I would never go for that."

"Are you sure, Mom? It's a really cool gadget. My buddy's mom has one, and she loves it."

"That's great. I'm happy for her."

"So you're certain you don't want one?"

"I'm sure. And son?"

"Yeah, Mom?"

"Thanks for checking in with me first."

"Absolutely, Mom."

That same year on Boxing Day, a friend made her usual call to check in with me. "Hi Louise, how was your Christmas?"

"It was lovely. And yours?"

"Mine was great too. Oh, by the way, I walked one thousand steps today."

"Good on you!"

"Yeah, my daughter bought me this new gadget. It dings whenever I have met my goal."

"Sounds fun."

"You should get yourself one."

"I was offered one last Mother's Day. And I declined."

"They're really cool. My friend has one, and she uses it all the time."

I nodded and smiled. "Uh huh."

Undaunted, my well-meaning friend persisted. "Lou, it even measures your heart rate!"

"Oh my," I replied.

"And it tells you when you get a text. How smart is that?"

"My friend, that is the *last* thing I would want to know while out walking."

"Good for you, Louise. You know what you like and don't like."

*****

So there you have it. My unpopular opinion when it comes to the latest gadget. And should the day come when folks are keen to wear this technology inside their bodies, I'll be running the other way. Fast.

Musing #27: Night Owl

***

"*I often think that the night is more alive and more richly colored than the day.*"

— *Vincent Van Gogh*

Night Owl

Which one are you: an early bird or a night owl?

"I see you're not an early riser. I need a woman who wakes up early."
The man had explored my profile, and clearly, my sleeping habits did
not please him.

Best not to waste his time.

"Thank you for your observation. I wish you all the best in searching
for that special someone."

Twenty-four hours later, I detected he had checked my profile yet again. Several times.

Interesting, I thought, Mr. Early Bird may be having second thoughts. I know I'm not.

Ever since I can remember, I've always been a night owl.

As a kid, it was tough to live this way. Catching the 7:30 a.m. school bus was the worst part of my day. Eating breakfast was the last thing on my mind. Especially as I would wake up mere minutes before darting out the door.

Growing up, night skiing was my favourite. So few skiers were out on the trails past dinner time. And I could brood by myself with fewer distractions.

I love nighttime.

And I love it even more when I am left undisturbed.

Musing #28: Travel Lightly

❧

"On a long journey, even a straw weighs heavy."
— Spanish proverb

Travel Lightly

Stop the world! I want to get off.

When I suffered a nervous breakdown in my early thirties, I knew something had to change.

And it had to begin with me.

So I took an inventory:

- How am I spending my time?
- How do I feel about how I am spending my time?
- What do I need to cut out?
- What needs to stay?

Fast forward to 2022.

Now, when my world threatens to spin out of control, I put on the brakes.

You asked, "What is your opinion on simplifying? Why do you feel that way?"

You bet I believe in simplifying. And I can be pretty stubborn about this topic.

What does that look like for me?

I don't feel:

- obligated to own more than I need
- pressured to purchase what others possess
- pushed to modernize

Liberty is the word to describe it.

I have freedom from tyranny to:

- have more
- be more
- do more
- keep more
- say more
- control more

Life is complicated enough.

The last thing I desire is more clutter to weigh me down.

Thirteen moves over four years have certainly taught me this. So, yes. I am all into simplifying my life.

And what is the driving force behind it?

It's my hunger for space.

The kind that makes room for the things that really matter in my life.

Musing #29: Something Smells Fishy

"Our greatest freedom is the freedom to choose our attitude."
— Viktor E. Frankl

Something Smells Fishy

When you were a child, what did your parents send to school for your lunches?

Preparing school lunches was one of my chores.

And with six siblings, that called for a lot of bread. No wonder Mom bought more than forty loaves each week.

I was granted three options for sandwiches:

1. Peanut butter
2. Jam

3. Peanut butter and jam

All on white Pan-Dandy bread.

Throw in an apple. Plus, two cookies.

And lunch was made.

One time, I prepared baloney sandwiches for everyone.

Bad decision.

When the lunch bell rang, those sandwiches smelled sour. (We didn't have the thermal lunch bags you can buy today to keep food chilled.)

When I started school in grade 1, Mom always made our school lunches.

I'll never forget the day I clicked open my tin lunch kit. Mom had made a new kind of sandwich. A gooey Cheez Whiz sandwich. The taste was different than anything I had ever had before. It was salty and bitter. And it left a chemical taste in my mouth.

An hour later, I felt sick to my stomach.

Thankfully, Mom soon grew tired of the stuff and never bought it again. And I was happy to stick with peanut butter. And jam.

Or both.

Musing #30: Honest to Goodness

"Love doesn't mean doing extraordinary or heroic things. It means
knowing how to do ordinary things with tenderness."
— Jean Vanier, Community and Growth

Honest to Goodness

Have you ever known someone who was scammed? Have you ever had to help that person, especially if they were elderly?

My dear late father-in-law was in his early nineties when his beloved bride died. With Mom no longer managing the bills, Dad looked to me for help.

One day, the phone rang. It was Dad. "Lou, can you talk to those people on the phone? I can't understand a word they say." Dad was very hard of hearing. And his hearing aids were unreliable.

I hollered into the receiver, "Dad, I'll be right over."

Upon arrival, Dad handed me the monthly bills from the telephone company. "Lou, what are all these charges for?"

I switched on the desk lamp and scoured the papers. I noticed a repeated charge. Something about long-distance administrative fees kept popping up.

"Dad, may I call these people on your behalf?" Dad nodded.

Once on the phone, I explained who I was and why I was calling.

"May we speak with your father?" the voice said.

"Dad, they want to talk to you."

Dad turned up his hearing aids and pressed the receiver against his ear. "Yes, I give my daughter permission to speak for me. Do what she says. Please." Poor man. He was so overwhelmed.

I took the phone and asked to speak with a supervisor. A few moments later, another voice came on the line, the supervisor.

I said, "I have examined my father's telephone bills for the last twelve months. Apparently, he is being charged for a service he never requested. He never makes long-distance calls. He has no interest in making long-distance calls. And he never granted permission to be charged a fee he does not need."

I continued, "I need to hear from you today that you will reimburse my father for all these fees dating back to when they began. Please assure me you will carry out this request immediately."

By the end of the conversation, Dad was a few hundred dollars richer.

"A cup of tea, Dad?" Dad smiled, and I put on the kettle and made a pot of Earl Grey tea.

"Lou, can you help me with my credit card statements too? I see some charges there that I don't remember making."

"For sure, Dad," I replied. At that, big crocodile tears poured down his cheeks.

"Thank you, Lou. You are a true daughter."

"You've been there for me, Dad. And I'm here for you today."

So yes, I did have to step in and help an elderly relative who was being scammed. More than once. And in my case, I am thankful that Dad never once fought me on this. On the contrary, he trusted me 100 per cent to carry out his wishes.

Money cannot buy that level of trust.

Musing #31: All Dolled Up

"You are you. Now, isn't that pleasant?"
— Dr. Seuss

All Dolled Up

Why don't you wear makeup?

The quick answer is that makeup and me just don't get along.

The only makeup I habitually wore was stage makeup in high school drama class. I think the pencils were #9 and #5.

I was in my mid-teens when my childhood friend persuaded me to submit to a makeover.

"Lou, you'll love the new look. Just wait and see!" How brave she was trying out that experiment with me.

110

"Ouch!"

"Lou! Hold still."

"How long does this take?"

I imagined torture was better than this.

Thirty minutes later, my friend put down her brush and announced, "Oh, Louise, you are bee-u-tee-full! Go look in the mirror."

I hunted for my eyeglasses and stepped in front of the vanity mirror.

"Help! Who is that?" The person in the mirror was not me. Not by a long shot.

"Do you like it?" I glanced at my friend and caught the hope in her eyes.

"No! I'm sorry! Please, take this off me *now*!"

"Okay, Lou! Just hold on."

Within minutes, I could breathe easy. And much to my relief, I recognized myself again in the mirror.

Back in time:

When I was about eight, we would take Smarties (a candy similar to M&Ms) and lick them, one at a time. Then we would use those as makeup.

We went out night skiing with our green eye shadow, pink cheeks, and red lips from the dye in the Smarties. Nobody ever made fun of us or said a word.

What a hoot!

Musing #32: Smoke and Mirrors

"Don't trust everything you see. Even salt looks like sugar."
— Unknown

Smoke and Mirrors

Right from the get-go, she should have smelled a rat. But she ignored it.

Why is that?

She wanted to believe he was the real meal deal. That he was who he said he was. That she was indeed high on his priority list.

Big mistake.

And yet, here she is. Learning from life's lessons.

And that's a good thing.

So, you asked, "What was the most important lesson you learned from heartbreak?"

Here are eleven lessons I learned.

After the fact:

1. Never ignore a red flag.
2. Never minimize a suspicion that something is very wrong.
3. Never apologize for something you did not do.
4. Never permit someone else to control you.
5. Never allow anyone to trample on your values and beliefs.
6. Never give up on yourself.
7. Never say yes when you mean no.
8. Never let someone treat you like a child.
9. Never believe you are unworthy of respect.
10. Never assume that forgiving someone means you must reconcile.
11. Finally, never ever lose hope.

Oh, and one more . . .

Call it for what it was: Smoke and mirrors.

Musing #33: Charity Begins at Home

❧❧❧

"He who has pity on the poor lends to the Lord, And He will pay back what he has given." — Proverbs 19:17 NKJV

Charity Begins at Home

The woman glanced up from her tray and noticed him.

Watching her from afar.

She looked down at her fries. Picked up her $1.50 coffee and sipped.

And pondered.

Who is this man?

And what is his story?

She glanced over one more time. His gaze never left her.

Another man sat down. Not too far away. He looked at the man who was studying her. And then turned his head and examined her.

Now, she was intrigued.

All this body language. And no one is saying a word.

She gobbled her last fry and took one last sip. And looked around for a wastebasket.

And contemplated some more.

A busboy wiped a table nearby.

Can you help me, please? The young man nodded.

See that gentleman sitting by the window? He is resting his head down on the table.

Yes, I see him, replied the clerk.

May I order a meal and pay for it now, and you serve it to him when it is ready?

The young man smiled and nodded, yes.

He was no more than high school age.

That's very kind of you, said the clerk.

She smiled. It's the right thing to do.

The young man guided the woman to the order kiosk. And there, she decided on what to serve the gentleman.

Something easy to chew. Protein. Carbs. And coffee to go.

May I be assured you will serve the meal to him when it is cooked?

Yes, I will be happy to do that.

Thank you. Thank you so much.

So, back to your question. You asked, "How does adversity reinforce humility?"

Many of us know what it feels like to be hungry, tired, lonely and afraid.

And yes, homeless too.

That gentleman gave her a gift that day. A reminder of how blessed she was with the kindness of others.

And that in itself was very humbling.

Somehow, she believed that had that been her. Sitting and staring. He would have done the same for her.

Musing #34: Happy Camper

~꧁꧂~

"But Jesus said, 'Let the little children come to Me, and do not
forbid them; for of such is the kingdom of heaven.'"
— *Matthew 19:14 NKJV*

Happy Camper

My toddler grandson peeked out from behind the couch. His eyes grew wide.

- Forget the blocks.
- Forget the crayons.
- Forget the plastic jungle animals.

Gŭmma Yū?

Yes?

Did you get theeez boxes for me?

I sure did.

The little man does a happy dance.

Yayyyyyy!

You asked, "What is your best tip to live a happy life?"

My best tip would be . . .

Never lose the joy that childlike wonder brings.

Musing #35: Pee My Pants

"To live is so startling it leaves little time for anything else."
— *Emily Dickinson*

Pee my Pants

Has a book ever made you laugh so hard that you fell off your chair?

My teenage daughter hollered from her bedroom, "Mom! *What* are you reading?"

Back in those days, I was raising children.

Youngsters who needed to study.

And sleep.

Who preferred their mom not to act so silly.

What mother do you know laughs so hard she almost pees her pants while reading a book?

Yep. That's me.

That is when I read Erma Bombeck, my all-time first choice for a hilarious read.

I first discovered Erma Bombeck when I entered premature menopause at age thirty-one. She understood what it's like to have a hot flash. At work. While wearing pantyhose.

Gosh, I'm sweating bricks just thinking about it.

Once I got a hold of her books, I could not put them down.

I am laughing right now as I remember my favourite titles, all by Erma Bombeck:

- The Grass Is Always Greener over the Septic Tank
- If Life Is a Bowl of Cherries, What Am I Doing in the Pits?
- I Lost Everything in the Post-Natal Depression
- Just Wait until You Have Children of Your Own
- When You Look Like Your Passport Photo, It's Time to Go Home

Here's what I just realized about Erma: she had this uncanny ability to reframe life experiences and see the humour in the most mundane things.

Musing #36: Leaving Home

﹋

"Hope itself is like a star- not to be seen in the sunshine of prosperity, and only to be discovered in the night of adversity."
— Charles H. Spurgeon

Louise @ 17 - One Year after Leaving Home

Circa 1974: Two weeks after graduating from high school.

Her pink curlers bobbled as she studied me up and down. "How old did you say you are?"

"I'm sixteen."

"I hope you're not a runaway. Are these all your things?"

I swallowed hard. "Yes. And no, I'm not a runaway."

I handed her my first month's rent. Four twenty-dollar bills quickly disappeared down her bra. "No shenanigans, you hear?"

I nodded.

The interview was over.

I hauled Alexander, my ten-speed bicycle, up the three flights of stairs. A thin woman peeked out from her room. I smiled. One look and she slammed her door shut. Click! Her deadbolt latched in place.

Next-door neighbours were sure different here in the city. Where I came from, no one locked their doors. People waved when you passed by.

Not here.

Welcome to the city of Ottawa.

Where summers are humid, and the air is heavy. Beads of sweat poured down my back. I glanced down at my key. Room #34.

I located my room at the end of the long, narrow hall. One turn, and the deadbolt clicked open. I stepped in and surveyed the room. A window at one end, a small closet, and three pieces of furniture.

128

I leaned Alexander against the wall and tossed my knapsack onto the bare mattress. A bare wood dresser with splotches and an old kitchen chair lined the opposite wall.

"I need air!"

The window stuck. Two more pushes, and it creaked open. I poked my head through and studied Bank Street below.

Buses, cars, and trucks weaved through the busy street. Fumes hung in the air.

My nose burned.

"Hot dogs! Donuts!" A short bald man with a greasy apron hollered to passersby. It was lunchtime. Men dressed in suits and ties crammed food into their mouths and glanced at their watches.

A woman with no teeth reached into a garbage can.

Girls in spike heels and fishnet stockings tarried at the street corner.

A teenager zigzagged through the crowd. "Boom! Ba da boom! Boom," went the boom box on his shoulders. The echo of drums bounced from building to building like a pinball machine.

You asked, "What is the most moving poem you have ever read?"

Well, that was the moment I grasped the meaning behind the words of my favourite poem:

"Lurid and lofty and vast it seems;
    It hath no rounded name that rings,
    But I have heard it called in dreams
    The City of the End of Things."[1]

What fresh hell had I just moved into?

My journey as an adult had now begun.

At sixteen years of age.

---

[1] Archibald Lampman, "The City of the End of Things," (Public Domain), Bartleby, accessed November 17, 2022, https://www.bartleby.com/246/1241.html.

Musing #37: A Room with a View

"GOTTA GO!" — *Words on a tombstone, British Columbia, Canada*

A Room with a View

Would you enter a cemetery by yourself at night?

In jest, I tell my friends and family, "I own oceanfront property." And then I explain it is a small piece of land, quite modest.

We're talking maybe two by two feet wide.

Something like that.

It's a cremation plot. And it is located in a lovely rural setting. On a small island.

By the sea.

Now, would I enter a cemetery by myself at night?

Yes. I would. And I have.

And it is one of the most peaceful places on earth.

At one point, I wanted my children to scatter my ashes into the ocean. But I later decided against it. Good thing too. It's windy near the ocean in this part of the world.

Ashes + Wind = A potential disaster.

Those ashes might blow back all over my children.

That wouldn't be so pleasant.

Nope. Not for me.

Into the ground I go. Nicely tucked into my handmade urn.

The one fashioned with wood from my birthplace.

Yes. It is lovely to walk through that country cemetery.

Day or night.

And it's not scary at all.

At least not where I will be buried.

Under a mature arbutus or oak tree. Can't recall which one.

I like the idea that a morning robin might just sing in that tree.

Each and every morning. And at dusk.

My favourite time of day.

This is my idea of a great resting place.

Until I am called home to Heaven, that is.

Now, I must say, *that* will be the perfect place to be at rest.

Musing #38: Sleep on It

❧

"Little by little, one travels far." — J. R. R. Tolkien

Sleep on It

What memory stands out to you the most from your school days?

"Mom!"

"What's wrong, Louise?"

"I keep forgetting my lines!"

"Now, here's what you do."

Mom's paring knife pointed towards the memory cards in my hand.

"Tonight, before you go to bed, read your speech one more time. Put your cards under your pillow. And as soon as you wake up, read your speech again."

My face flushed with tears. "Okay, Mom."

"And Louise?"

"Yes, Mom?"

"You'll do great."

Mom was right. I did do great. On the second try.

An unforgettable night.

The night I won my first and only trophy.

With a little help from my mom.

Musing #39: Days Gone By

***

"I always look forward to rewarding myself with the small pleasure of getting back to my typewriter and writing something."
— *Isaac Asimov*

Days Gone By

Do you miss using a manual typewriter?

Uncle Ziggy gave me a lovely little typewriter. It came with its own case. That typewriter went everywhere with me.

Even camping. Like when Dad took us to Cape Breton Island for summer holidays.

I can see myself now.

Sitting at a picnic table at Corney Brook Campground and banging out my next edition of *Just a Little* newspaper. We had no electricity at that campsite. Made no difference to me. Not with my trustworthy portable typewriter!

Now, back to your question.

You asked, "Do you miss using a manual typewriter?"

I confess I miss the crash of the return bar. How dramatic! It felt like I was making a powerful statement.

And the zzzzz the roller made when you inserted a piece of paper.

Oh, and the clickety-clack of the keys.

How my fingers flew!

Oh, and remember typing class?

I really liked Mrs. Black. She let me sit at the back of the class. Near the door. Right opposite a sweet boy. With an even sweeter grin. Gosh, he made me laugh.

Did you know that laughter helps learning?

It sure did for me. And still does.

Yep. I loved typing class. It was my favourite class in grade 8.

Oh, and I almost forgot . . . the *ding ding* of the bell!

Musing #40: Lost at Sea

❧❦❧

"Grief is not a disorder, a disease or sign of weakness. It is an
emotional, physical and spiritual necessity, the price you pay for
love. The only cure for grief is to grieve."
— Earl A. Grollman

Lost at Sea

Is it unhealthy to stuff your emotions?

"When Mordecai got wind of an evil plot to have all Jews murdered, he tore his clothes, put on sackcloth and ashes, and went out into the city, wailing loudly and bitterly." (Esther 4:1, my paraphrase).

Grief does that to a person. And it's not pretty.

Upon hearing her uncle's public display of emotion, Queen Esther sent clean clothes with these instructions. "Get up. Wash your face. And change your clothes."

In other words, "Be quiet."

Not long ago, I allowed myself to grieve in the presence of a friend. My grief was a mixture of fury and frustration. Anger against the mass deception and distress, knowing nothing could be done.

Add to that, a few choice (my bad) F-bombs, and well, it was not pretty.

Sorrow can do that to a person.

Especially to someone who feels deeply.

Whether it be mirth. Or misery.

You asked, "Is it unhealthy to stuff your emotions?"

Had Mordecai not expressed his raw emotions that day, Esther would not have gotten wind of the wicked plot to destroy her people. And an entire nation would have been annihilated.

In my case, I learned to be careful with whom I open up to about my own grief. Not everyone can handle ugly emotions. They can scare some and offend others.

As for mourning, give me an ash heap any day. I cannot and will not suppress my sorrow. No matter how ugly it may look.

Musing #41: Coming Home

⸎

"Yes, I believe in Heaven. Real life hasn't begun yet.
All of this is just shadows." — C. S. Lewis in Shadowlands

Coming Home (Photo courtesy of my son - Permission granted)

Do you believe in life after death?

My dad was talking with me. Alone. My dad who normally said very little. My WWII and Korean War veteran Dad.

"Lou, I saw my body lying there in the hospital room. I was looking down. From the corner at the ceiling. I felt no pain. The doctor and nurses were trying to revive me."

"Gosh, Dad."

"And then, suddenly, I left the room and saw a bright light. And then, I was back in my body. And I felt terrible pain in my chest."

Dad wanted very much to share his experience with me. His middle child. The one who had religion.

Several years later, my dad called me out of the blue. On his birthday. It was extraordinary that he would call. He was alone in a hospital room. On the other side of Canada. He was fighting cancer.

And losing.

And gaining something even more precious.

"Lou, there was nothing to read except a Gideon Bible that I found in the drawer beside my bed. So I started reading."

"That's so cool, Dad. Where did you start reading?"

"Well, with page one, of course!"

I smiled through the phone and pictured my dad sitting up in bed, alone in a hospital room. With one book. A book he had scorned and shunned for his entire life.

A few months later, my sister-in-law called. "Lou, your dad is dying." Dad's cancer had returned. He was now paralyzed from the chest down. And in terrible pain.

I took a red-eye flight that very day. Clear across the country from Victoria, British Columbia, to Cape Breton Island, Nova Scotia.

I prayed I would have a moment alone with him. And that he would be lucid.

"Lou! How long are you here for?"

"As long as I need to be, Dad. I did not book a return flight home." Dad reached for my hand and held on tight. He would not let go.

That afternoon, he asked, "Lou, can I talk with you about spiritual matters?"

"Absolutely, Dad."

We talked at length. One moment, laughing, and the next, sniffling with tears.

"Dad, do you know for certain that if you died tonight, you would be with God in Heaven?"

"No, Lou! I don't know that. And I want to!"

"Would you like me to pray with you, Dad?"

Dad smiled through his tears. "Yes, Lou. Would you?"

That day, I met my dad for the very first time. My real dad. The man with the little boy heart who cried out to his Papa in Heaven. The man who asked his God for forgiveness. The man who, on that day, decided he wanted to go Home.

You might wonder, "Do you believe in life after death?"

Dear reader, I most certainly do. This life on earth is but a blip in eternity. How do I know this?

It all begins with a seed of faith. Faith that believes that surely you were created with eternity in your heart.

Do I believe?

Oh my. That is exactly what is keeping me grounded in a world mired in grief and sorrow. I look beneath my feet. And what do I see? A firm foundation. One that cannot be shaken. Not by pestilence. Not by fear. Not by tyranny. And not by death.

I so look forward to returning to the Garden. A place where moths, dust, and rust never corrupt. No decay. No more tears. And no more sorrow.

Only laughter. Freedom. Catching up with cherished companions and family. And joy. Unspeakable joy.

Musing #42: Blowing Smoke

❧

"Propaganda works best when those who are being manipulated
are confident they are acting on their own free will."
— Joseph Goebbels

Blowing Smoke

How do you know if someone is lying to you?

Short answer?

I question everything.

When I was eighteen years old, I decided to enrol in a business marketing program at a local college. It seemed practical. Reasonable.

And promised a measure of job security. Remember, I had left home at sixteen. I needed a way to support myself.

Enter advertising.

Though I was doing well academically, I became increasingly uneasy. I started to ask pointed questions in class.

- Why introduce a product that no one needs?
- Why sell it in such a way that it creates a voracious hunger?
- Isn't that wrong?
- Isn't that sneaky?

I learned how advertisers can manipulate through hidden and blatant messages.

I looked around me and wondered, "Doesn't anyone see a problem here?"

Call it a dis-ease.

I refused to buy into that kind of deception. The kind that renders you powerless to think rationally. The kind that takes advantage of others.

Without their knowledge.

Oh, and about the program I was enrolled in?

I quit.

Musing #43: At the End of the Day

❧

"Faithless is he that says farewell when the road darkens."
— *J.R.R. Tolkien*, The Fellowship of the Ring

"Mom, should I even bother visiting Grandpa? He just falls asleep."

"And when Grandpa wakes up, whose face does he see?"

"Well, mine."

"And each time Grandpa wakes up during your visit, he knows you will be there. Ready to chat or make another cup of tea."

My teenaged son thought for a long time. "So, even if I don't think it's productive, it is for Grandpa?"

"It sure is. He looks forward to each and every visit with you. One day, when Grandpa is no longer with us, you will look back and never, ever regret making time for him."

To this day, I am grateful for how my children made time for their Grandma and Grandpa.

- Even when they were active teenagers.
- Even when they were travelling the world.
- Even when they were in college.

One day, you, too, will be your grandparents' age.

A day will come when you are less mobile and more fatigued. You will begin to notice the obituary page as more of your friends die. You will feel more and more vulnerable as you lose the ability to run like the wind.

154

And when that day comes, you will welcome each and every visit a loved one pays you.

- Even when you fall asleep.
- Even when they wonder, "Is this worthwhile?"

And during this time of upheaval, when you may not have the privilege of visiting Grandma and Grandpa in person, they are just a phone call away. Or you could even send a card through snail mail.

Musing #44: Monkey Business

"I have had a wonderful time but this wasn't it."
— *Groucho Marx*

Monkey Business

What are some funny pick-up lines you've heard?

I was again single and in my fifties when I signed up for an online dating site. Four men come to mind. Each with their own memorable opening lines.

157

Mr. Coffee Man:

"Hey, Gorgeous! You're too young to be on this site. How about you and me meet for coffee? Blimey, I gotta get off this dating site!"

The man lived on the other side of the country.

Mr. Movie Man:

"Do you like action movies?"

"Sometimes, yes. I like many genres."

"Good. Let's go to the movies tomorrow."

"How about we get acquainted first?"

Poof. Mr. Movie Man disappeared.

Mr. Boat Man:

"You like boats?"

"Yes, I like boats."

"I live on a boat."

"That's nice."

"You want to go for a boat ride this weekend?"

Suddenly, I remembered I get seasick when bathing in large tubs. I also imagined being thrown overboard in the middle of the ocean.

That was the end of that plan.

Mr. Talk-Dirty Man:

"Hey, Beautiful. Wanna talk dirty on the phone?"

"No, thank you."

I should have told him what Groucho Marx said, "I have had a wonderful time but this wasn't it."

Musing #45: Crash and Burn

﹡◦◦◦﹡

"One of the tragedies of our life is that we keep forgetting who we are." — Henri J.M. Nouwen, Here and Now: Living in the Spirit

Crash and Burn

What does self-care look like to you?

Once upon a time, I did not understand self-care.

That is, until I crashed and burned.

I declare, my boss never slept. He was the last to leave and the first to arrive in the morning. He also expected me to do the same.

One eventful morning:

"Louise, meet me in my office in five minutes. And let's change the

161

world!"

He took one look at my red eyes. "What's wrong?"

"I don't know," I whimpered. "I can't stop crying." I was a mess. And here I was, the administrator, and I couldn't even remember who I had just telephoned.

He shook his head. "Go home, Louise."

I sobbed all the way home and went straight to bed. There I lay, weeping. For days. Then I slept. For several more days. My husband was beside himself. We had a mortgage to pay and two small children to feed.

"Louise, we need you to go back to work. We have expenses."

And that's when I sank even deeper.

Call it a sinkhole. The darkness was so thick. I could not breathe.

"I can't go back there. Please. Please try again to find work."

I was the primary breadwinner. Not by choice. By necessity. We had recently moved thousands of miles out west, where my husband had received two job offers. But upon arrival in the new city, the proposals had fallen through.

My dream of being a stay-at-home mom ended.

Two weeks later, I gave my high-energy boss a full six months' notice.

My husband found work. And I got to be a stay-at-home mom for a few years.

Ever so slowly, I crawled out from my despair.

Four years later, I discovered the book, *Boundaries: When to Say Yes, How to Say No to Take Control of Your Life,* by Drs. Cloud and Townsend. I joined a 12-step recovery support group and started to see a psychotherapist.

Coming home to ourselves takes courage and hard work.

And yes, it is so worth it.

How so?

When you discover who you truly are and how you are made, that's when you come home to yourself.

No longer a stranger but very much a friend.

Here are seven self-care tips I learned along the way:

1. Purchase an alarm clock for every member of the family. And stop playing rescuer when others are late for work or school.
2. Mount a key rack on the wall next to the front door. And stop hunting for everyone else's keys.
3. Start delegating chores each day to other family members. And stop trying to do it all.
4. Screen your calls. That's what caller ID is for. In fact, turn your phone off. The world won't end if you miss a call.

5. Start showing love and respect for yourself. Ask yourself daily, "What is one way I can care for myself today?"
6. Schedule family meetings once a week. Start addressing any concerns.
7. Begin asking yourself, "How do I feel?" and "What do I need?"

And remember, self-care is not selfish.

Musing #46: Come Rain or Shine

"To every thing there is a season, and a time to every purpose under the heaven: A time to be born, and a time to die; a time to plant, and a time to pluck up that which is planted."
— *Ecclesiastes 3:1-2 NKJV*

Come Rain or Shine

How do I plan for end-of-life matters?

I told my executor, "Just look for the red box."

What's in the red box?

1. A copy of my revised will
2. A copy of my prepaid funeral plans
3. A copy of my prepaid cremation plot location
4. A copy of all my passwords (Yes, I have different passwords for every account.)
5. A copy of my credit card and other significant cards
6. A copy of my Vital Stats information
7. A copy of my professional associations
8. A copy of my car registration/insurance papers

9. A copy of my personal and end-of-life wishes
10. Other important stuff I can't think of right now
11. And when I get around to it, personal last letters to my loved ones

I want a cake (something with lemon) ordered in and decorated with the little plastic figures I once used on my children's cakes when they were little.

Why cake and nothing else?

I don't want folks to go to a lot of fuss. Instead, I want them to enjoy something simple at my celebration-of-life service. Oh, and I would like Tim Horton's coffee to be served.

Regular. Not dark roast. Fussy girl, am I.

Why?

Because their coffee tastes great and is simple to order in. Again, simplicity. That's the word of the day.

Gosh, you might call it a minimalist's version of a funeral service.

I was born into a French Canadian family, where we are not afraid to discuss death.

Now, back to the red box.

My urn was purchased some time ago. And it, too, is tucked away in the red box. It was created out of wood from my hometown of Wakefield, Québec. My childhood best friend's hubby, Brian Cross, crafted it.

I can't prepare for all that life will throw at me.

But I can do what I can ahead of time.

And that is good enough for me.

Musing #47: Red Herring

"Courage is the art of being the only one who knows you are scared to death." — Earl Wilson

Red Herring

What steps should a person take to leave an abusive relationship?

Play dumb. Clam up. And smile.

Start a pretend diary.

And fill it with platitudes.

Do not speak of the nightmare you are living anywhere in the pages of that journal. Do not write what you are really feeling.

Honesty could put you in harm's way.

Leave the journal sitting on your desk. He will probably read it when you are away from the house. That diary can serve as a decoy.

And while certain parties might dig into and take photos of your belongings without your permission, you can quietly gather documentation.

And get your ducks in a row.

Once you have what you need, leave.

Then, disappear.

Recommended Reading:
Why Does He Do That?: Inside the Minds of Angry and Controlling Men, by Lundy Bancroft

Musing #48: See the Full Picture

*"The two most important days of your life are the day you are born
and the day you find out why." — Anonymous*

See the Full Picture

What did I learn later in life that changed my world?

"Your maternal grandfather only spoke *Jargon*, Louise."

"What's *Jargon*, Mom?"

"It's a mix of Native and French."

My eyes grew wide, "Are you saying we have Algonquin blood in our veins? Mom! That's amazing!"

So that makes me French Canadian (or Québécois), Irish, and Algonquin. As you probably know, I like to answer questions by telling a story. Turns out these three cultures all honour the storytelling tradition.

Okay, so where does that leave me today?

I am slowly learning to integrate my worldview while honouring my cultural heritage.

How do I do that?

By listening.

- To the beat of my own heart,
- To the wind in the trees and the birds of the air,
- To the Holy Spirit, as He speaks to me through His Word and in my dreams at night,
- And to music when I must weep, dance, worship, or pray.

Despite the oppression my ancestors experienced at the residential schools, I thank God they were never obliterated from the face of the earth.

Like them, I, too, will persevere.

And I will learn lessons from my ancestors as I move forward.

One day at a time.

Afterword:

My daughter is the one who first declared my gift as a storyteller. And it was she who connected the dots regarding my cultural heritage. Without this discovery, I doubt I would have the courage to write and draw as I do.

Musing #49: Light Bulb Moment

❧❦❧

"Today you are You, that is truer than true. There is no one alive who is Youer than You." — Dr. Seuss

Light Bulb Moment

My church history professor posed the question, "What do you think about this? Or, how does this make you feel?"

I tell you when I heard him use the word "feel," I was over the moon.

You mean, my feelings about this topic are relevant as well?

Thinking and feeling.

At that time, I had no idea I was (am) primarily right-brained.

I feel things out before I think about them.

As I previously discussed and explain in greater detail at the end of this book, I'm an HSP (highly sensitive person). I feel deeply about the things that matter to me.

I can now appreciate how that one question forty years ago so resonated with me. Logic, for me, takes time to process. It's a lot of work.

And it is not my strength.

Ask me to process through my values, and I am on board.

I prefer to think, talk, write, and draw in a circular fashion. Kinda like what a storyteller might do. Linear thinking is not my strength.

So what is the best writing prompt I have ever been asked by a teacher?

That one question changed the course of history for me.

The day I discovered I was not deficient.

Not handicapped and most certainly not backward.

I am okay, just the way God made me.

Musing #50: Silence is Golden

"In solitude we wait for all the noise to quiet in order to find out what we are really thinking about." — Joan Chittister, The Gift of Years: Growing Older Gracefully

Silence is Golden

What are the benefits of silence?

"Louise, come out of your room and say hello."

"Okayyyy, Mom!"

Dear Mom. She was a considerable extrovert who had a wonderful gift of hospitality. The more people in the house, the merrier she was.

Only for me, it often felt like Grand Central Station. People would come and go at all hours of the day. If I wasn't holed up in my room, I was hiding somewhere.

Fast forward to recent times . . .

As an adult, I decide when I want to hang out with family and friends and when I need to retreat to a quiet place.

Solitude and silence are gifts I value highly.

And fortunately for me, I now have heaps of opportunity to retreat and refresh.

Like when I spent a night in a rustic log cabin up in Peace River Country, Alberta, with Vanesa, my dear friend from college.

(Written Fall 2019)

At the cabin, I open the door.

And gaze up at the moon.

How she shimmers in the treetops.

And dozes above the mist below.

Stillness.

An owl hoots.

A mosquito whines.

In the pitch-black cabin, I reach for the latch and close the door.

I grope for the side table.

Place my eyeglasses.

And feel for the bed.

I pull back the covers.

Cotton sheets crackle between my fingers.

I climb into bed.

Moonlight pours through the open window.

A clock on the wall comes alive.

Tick tock. Tick tock.

Its melody matches my breath.

Is that a rustle I hear in the walls?

Ahh yes. Mice.

They do come alive at night.

I strain to hear.

Tick tock. Tick Tock.

Swish, swish, whispers the breeze in the trees.

What are the benefits of silence?

- peace
- stillness
- calm
- simplicity

No clutter.

No complications.

Oh, the gift of silence.

What is its message for me tonight?

A chapter has fully closed.

A new story has just begun.

Musing #51: Bad Egg

~~~oୠo~~~

"Sometimes the questions are complicated and the answers are simple." — Dr. Seuss

Bad Egg

What did I learn from previous relationships?

I met some good and bad eggs in my late teens and earlier twenties.
    The good eggs were really good eggs.

And because I was a sick (and a gullible) egg, I had no idea that the good eggs were good for me. Sad how I saw them as ho-hum and humdrum.

Boring and blah.
    Looking back, they were anything but dull.

- These were wholesome men.
- Real men.

- Kind men.
- Devoted men.
- Gentle-men.

And they loved me to the moon and back.

Years later,

I wish I could ask for their forgiveness for messing with their affections.
　So what if I was angry at the world?
　That did not give me the right to throw them to the curb.

"Why do bad boys get all the girls?"
　Nasty boys know all the lines.

- "Where have you been all my life?"
- "I've never loved anyone like you."
- "You are my soul mate."
- "You're number one."

If I could do it all over again, I would have kissed the bad eggs goodbye, right from the start.

You asked, "What did you learn from previous relationships?"
　Short answer?
　It's never too late to say no to a bad egg. Ever.

Musing #52: Cold Sweat

~~~

"Beware of a wolf in sheep's clothing." — *Aesop*

Cold Sweat

Has someone ever used fear and intimidation against you?

This is a story from my teenage years. Back in 1975.

When I was seventeen.

I have met a few wolves in sheep's clothing. And sadly, I was vulnerable to their charms. And here I was, looking for love in all the wrong places.

One of those wolves seemed to be a lovely man, well-dressed and wearing expensive cologne. But he turned out to be a pimp. A brothel keeper who managed to lure me far away to a middle-of-nowhere, seedy hotel.

"We can go dancing after dinner," he said.

I had left home the year before and lived in the city.

Was I street-wise? You tell me.

Let's just say he had more than dinner and dancing in mind. Later that night, he introduced me to his "girls" in his hotel room.

I was sitting on a chair when his girls entered the room.

They began to swoon about me.

"Girl, your skin is *fine*. Let's make you up!"

They fussed with my long hair and twirled it with their fingers, invading my personal space. My skin began to crawl, and I wanted to heave.

I knew I was in danger big time.

The question was, how in the world would I get out of there when I had no car?

So I came up with a secret plan.

I waited.

Finally, his breathing grew heavy. I slipped out from under the sheets and slid towards the chair where my clothes lay. My bladder was ready to burst. But I couldn't risk it. I couldn't take a chance that he might wake up.

I groped in the dark, found my glasses, and slipped on my jeans and T-shirt. I grabbed my shoes with one hand and picked up my knapsack with the other.

The hallway light under the door was my beacon to safety.

I turned the knob and closed the door gently behind me.

And flew down the stairs.

Two steps at a time.

And landed in the hotel front lobby.

In those days, cell phones were unheard of. I sighed when I spotted a pay phone.

I whispered into the receiver, "A taxi, please. Right away."

An eternity later, a black taxi pulled up to the curb. "Where to, young lady?"

I leaned over the seat and handed the driver all my money. A twenty-dollar bill. I then gave him my address. An address I had not provided the pimp. An address no one in my family knew.

That was fortunate indeed. Because the next day, Mr. Pimp Man was seen strutting around my village, asking for Louise Gagné. In fact, he even went to the ski resort right next to my house. My Mom worked there.

"Does anyone know where I can find her?" he asked so innocently.

"Nope. Can't help you, sir. We don't know where Louise lives."

To think I could have taken a trip to Jamaica with that man (shiver). Someone was certainly looking out for me that day. I thank God for protecting me and delivering me from this evil, even though I didn't know Him then.

Musing #53: Sticks and Stones

"The only way to come to know where you are is to begin to make yourself at home." — George MacDonald, Lilith

Sticks and Stones

Have you ever binged on a whole pie or cake?

Quick answer? Yes.

I had a secret when I was a teen. And it filled me with shame.

From the age of twelve to nineteen, I was bulimic. And yes, some days, I was so out of control that I could eat a whole cake by myself. And once I was filled to the point where I could not stuff one more morsel in my mouth, I purged in secret.

How did this unhealthy behaviour start?

As I shared earlier, I was twelve when I revealed my fears that I was a monster to my mom.

You see, my body was developing, and I had no idea that this was completely normal. Mom was wise and knew I needed to hear from someone else that everything was as it should be.

And who better than a medical doctor?

Off to the big city, we went.

To see the doctor.

I was instructed to undress and put on a gown. Awkward and afraid, I climbed onto the examining table. The doctor poked and prodded here and there and then looked up.

"You can get dressed now," he said. "Please meet with me and your mother in my office."

I buttoned my blouse with trembling fingers. Minutes later, I rejoined my mother and the doctor.

"Louise, you are perfectly normal. Everything is as it should be."

I heaved a sigh of relief. Mom nodded. "See, I told you!"

And then the hammer fell.

"However, I recommend you lose five pounds."

Oh, no! Does that mean I am fat?

I remember standing at the curb, waiting for the light to turn green. At that moment, I decided to go on a diet. And lose those horrid five pounds.

Yes, I would start tomorrow.

That night, with no one watching, I tiptoed into the kitchen and devoured all the cookies in the tin, plus an entire bag of potato chips. I would stuff my face before the big diet was to begin.

Trouble was, the diet never really began. As a result, I soon developed a habit of bingeing and purging, bingeing and purging.

For seven years, that was how I coped.

And all that time, I never told a soul what I was doing.

All that time, I struggled with self-loathing and shame.

All that time, I felt ugly and fat.

I managed to stop when I was nineteen. Years later, I discovered the word bulimia. And you know what? If I am not mistaken, I read about it in a magazine article that addressed this eating disorder and gave a name to it.

So, yes. I have done that. Devoured whole pies and cakes.

Was that doctor right?

Was I overweight as a twelve-year-old?

No.

Not one single bit. If anything, I was slender and very muscular. In addition, I was always physically active: bicycling, hiking, swimming, canoeing, and skiing.

I wonder if the doctor thought I needed a goal to go home with.

Regrettably, little did he know how his words would scar me deeply.

Once the bulimia stopped, my body self-regulated, and I learned not to self-medicate with food. To this day, when I am hungry, I eat. And when I am full, I stop.

I cannot take one more bite.

I listen to my body.

My body is my friend. Not my enemy.

I am not a monster.

My body parts are normal.

I am normal.

Food is my friend. Not my enemy.

And I refuse to feel guilty for eating anything I choose to put in my mouth.

Musing #54: Look the Other Way

❧

"They say I'm old-fashioned, and live in the past, but sometimes I think progress progresses too fast!" — Dr. Seuss

Look the Other Way

Do we look at our phones when we feel bored or uncomfortable?

When you think of it, at one time, the makeup compact acted like today's flip phone.

We're talking in the early sixties.

I can see Aunt Tony now.

Rooting through her purse and pulling out red lipstick and a mirror.

1. Purse lips.
2. Apply.
3. Smack lips.
4. Apply again.

She had it down pat.

I get it now. Maybe it was Aunt Tony's way of bowing out of an awkward situation.

Or else she just loved her red lips.

Women don't do that as much anymore. Apply lipstick in public, I mean. At least not where I live. Everywhere I look, folks are looking down.

At their cell phones.

And it's not just women.

Anyone who has a phone.

So what did men do when they didn't want to engage? Before cell phones, that is?

Enter the newspaper.

The kind you hold with two hands. The kind you could hide behind. Dad regularly did this. Hid behind the pages. That was his go-to quiet place.

With seven kids in the house, Dad had to do something.

That or hide in his ham radio room in the basement.

Which he did later on.

As for me, I don't wear lipstick. And I rarely use my cell phone to avoid a conversation. I only turn it on when I have a chat date arranged. Or when I need to make a call. Put a book or newspaper in my hand, and I will open it. Every time.

Providing it's not rude to step away.

Social etiquette.

Quite the study.

Musing #55: Read You Loud and Clear

"A merry heart does good, like medicine,
But a broken spirit dries the bones." — Proverbs 17:22 NKJV

Read You Loud and Clear

What is your favourite childhood memory?

My Dad was a ham radio operator.

Not long after he built our home on the side of the ski hill at Edelweiss Valley, he set up his equipment in a little nook in our basement.

As I said before, he was a self-taught mechanical engineer.

Dad wanted to make contact with more operators. So he set up a taller radio ham tower on the roof. The result was fantastic: He was now getting great power and talking to hams clear across the Atlantic Ocean.

One night, I put toast in the toaster for a snack.

The toaster began to buzz. Then I heard Dad's voice in the toaster.

He was repeating his call sign!

I then plugged in the kettle for tea. And what do you know, Dad was now talking through the kettle as well!

"Dad," I yelled over the downstairs railing, "I can hear you talking in the toaster!"

Just then, the phone started ringing. "Dick! What's going on over there? We can hear you loud and clear in our television!"

Turns out several neighbours in the valley could hear Dad too.
  In *their* television.
  And they were not amused.

So Dad decided to go online in the wee hours of the night. When folks might not be preparing snacks or watching TV. Yep, Dad was a night owl, too, come to think of it.

My Dad was the consummate introvert, while my Mom was an extrovert who loved having people over. So his room was a place of escape.

I started showing interest in my Dad's hobby. That's when I discovered a new language called Morse Code. In my *Just a Little* newspaper, I introduced my readers to the language. I included the Morse Code alphabet and a secret message for readers to decipher.

At the dinner table, we had assigned seating. Everyone had a set place.

My place was beside Dad.

One day, I began to speak to him in Morse Code.

Dad broke out into a huge grin.

Someone was speaking his love language!

And you know something?

That was the sweetest conversation I ever had with my Dad at the dinner table.

Musing #56: Just Passing Through

"If I find in myself a desire which no experience in this world can satisfy, the most probable explanation is that I was made for another world." — *C. S. Lewis*, Mere Christianity

Just Passing Through (Louise, on January 19, 2023)

What do you say to give yourself hope during these dark times?

(Written in 2020)

I have felt deep grief these past several months.

Sometimes, weeping is the only way I know how to pray.

When did this begin?

This sorrow?

The day I woke up and saw it for what it was.

How life on this earth will never ever be the same.

My heart breaks for this broken world.

This abode that God once called good.

Oh, the Garden. How I long to return to the Garden.

What do I say to give myself hope during these dark times?

I remind myself I am but a *stranger* in this land.

And that soon. Yes, very soon,
   His Love will guide me Home.

———

"Thomas said to Him, 'Lord, we do not know where You are going, and how can we know the way?'
Jesus said to him, 'I am the way, the truth, and the life. No one comes to the Father except through Me.'" — John 14: 5-6 NKJV

Understanding a highly sensitive person (HSP)

In order to better understand some of the musings in this book, I have included some background and context on the personality trait of highly sensitive people or HSPs.

HSPs make up between 15 and 20 per cent of the population.

In general, HSPs have a personality trait that makes them, well, more sensitive to their environments and more easily overwhelmed by any type of external stimuli. However, people with HSP are not mentally ill although HSP can present with other mental health issues, such as anxiety or depression.

About 70 per cent of people with HSP are also introverts.[2]

---

[2] "Highly Sensitive Person," *Psychology Today*, accessed November 17, 2022, https://www.psychologytoday.com/us/basics/highly-sensitive-person.

HISTORY OF HSPs

In 1991, Dr. Elaine Aron began researching the phenomena of high sensitivity, also called sensory-processing sensitivity or SPS.[3] In 1996, she released a book, *The Highly Sensitive Person*, which provides excellent background on the subject.[4]

TRAITS OF HSPs

HSPs have the following traits:

- They are bothered by loud noises, bright lights, strong smells, or uncomfortable clothes.
- They do not like violence on TV or in the movies.
- They can be easily overwhelmed and then need quiet and privacy, preferably in a darkened room.
- They might be thought of as shy or sensitive.[5]
- They are deeply moved by nature, the human spirit, or art—any type of beauty.
- They are complex with deep thoughts and strong emotions, both positive and negative.[6]
- Many HSPs are very creative.[7]

---

[3] Aron, The Highly Sensitive Person.

[4] Elizabeth Scott, PhD, "What Is a Highly Sensitive Person (HSP)?" Very Well Mind, November 7, 2022, https://www.verywellmind.com/highly-sensitive-persons-traits-that-create-more-stress-4126393.

[5] Aron, The Highly Sensitive Person.

[6] Scott, "HSP?"

[7] "Highly Sensitive," *Psychology Today*.

- They might have a low tolerance for pain.[8]

Some cultures value sensitivity more than others. However, if the HSP is told, "Don't be so sensitive," they might struggle with low self-esteem.[9]

If your child has HSP, they might cry more easily. But they can do very well in the right environment.[10]

CAUSES OF HSP

The causes of HSP include early child experiences, hereditary factors, and environment. HSP can also be connected to experiencing trauma as a child. If other family members have HSP, you probably will too.[11]

However, the trait of HSP differs from other conditions: introversion, attention-deficit or hyperactivity disorder, autism, and sensory processing disorder. While there might be some overlapping of traits, HSP is a separate diagnosis. Sometimes, these other conditions can and do co-exist with HSP.

---

[8] Maté Jarai, "What is a Highly Sensitive Person?" Medical News Today, February 10, 2022, https://www.medicalnewstoday.com/articles/highly-sensitive-person#signs.

[9] Aron, The Highly Sensitive Person.

[10] "Highly Sensitive," *Psychology Today*.

[11] "Highly Sensitive," *Psychology Today*.

IMPACT OF LIFE ON AN HSP

HSPs might be easily hurt or overreact. When an HSP doesn't properly process their feelings, they might become aggressive, leading to further relationship or social challenges.

HSPs are not imagining interpersonal difficulties but are more sensitive to nuances between personalities and in relationships. As a result, HSPs might avoid overwhelming or highly stressful situations.

When they withdraw, they are not being antisocial but are simply aware of their own limits, which is a positive coping skill.

They may be especially thankful for a delicious meal or become extra emotional at an especially moving piece of music. They may have deep interpersonal relationships with others as they are very empathetic. Their empathy also makes them great candidates for leaders and managers. Lows may be lower, but highs may be higher.

HSPs especially struggle with hectic schedules, conflicts, self-criticism, and worry about letting people down. They have difficulty saying no and setting proper boundaries.

If a relationship ends, they overthink and worry about what they could have done differently to prevent the issue.

They may not deal with the basic stress of daily life well—traffic, getting angry when they are hungry, schedule delays. They tend to be perfectionists. They pick up on social cues others might miss, so they may have excellent social skills.[12]

STRATEGIES TO EFFECTIVELY DEAL WITH HSP

HSPs can learn effective life skills in order to effectively deal with this trait.

- Focus on positive aspects of life.
- Avoid or at least minimize stress.
- Work on setting boundaries and saying no.
- Make your home a safe space.[13]
- Be aware of your own personal needs and triggers.
- Focus on self-care.
- Declutter and minimize so that you aren't overwhelmed by too much stuff.
- Excellent coping strategies include a healthy diet, plenty of rest, moderate if any alcohol intake, and taking time off.[14]

In some cases, therapy can help HSPs cope more effectively, especially if they deal with depression, anxiety, or other mental health issues as well.

HSPs can also reduce sensory input in the following ways:

- Use physical devices, such as headphones, sunglasses, sleeping masks, ear plugs, etc.
- Buy comfortable clothes without seams or tags.

---

[12] Jarai, "What Is?"

[13] Scott, "HSP?"

[14] "Highly Sensitive," *Psychology Today*.

- Set up a quiet, dark room as a safe space in the house.[15]

CONCLUSION

If you or your child has HSP and does not realize it, life can be frustrating as you will interact with your environment and with family and friends differently than others might. You might feel as if you do not fit in or as if you are too sensitive. However, when an individual learns to properly deal with HSP, the trait turns into an asset and becomes less of a liability.

If you think you might have HSP, you can take the self-test at https://hsperson.com.

---

[15] Jarai, "What Is?"

About the Author

Louise D. (Gagné) Jewell grew up in a tiny village in rural Québec. She began her writing and illustrating career at fourteen as the editor and publisher of *Just a Little*, a community newspaper widely circulated in Edelweiss Valley, Wakefield, Québec, in the summer of 1973. She eventually obtained an MA in religion, graduating *magna cum laude* from Ambrose Seminary. And pursued further training in counselling psychotherapy from Providence Theological Seminary. Following the 2013 High River (Alberta) flood and the 2016 Fort McMurray (Alberta) wildfire, Louise served as a volunteer clinician providing psychosocial disaster services.

Louise's ancestors are French, Irish, and Algonquin, three cultures that honour the storytelling tradition that she carries on. As a writer, artist, retired registered clinical counsellor and betrayal trauma specialist, Louise is passionate about sharing her message of hope through story, both in written and visual form. Visit Louise's website at: www.louisejewellonline.com

Also by Louise D. Jewell

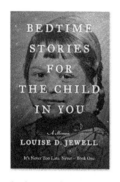

Bedtime Stories for the Child in You: A Memoir (Book One)
Louise shares precious memories of growing up in Wakefield, Québec. Colourful characters and comical stories along with Louise's whimsical illustrations help the reader identify with her journey. Whether she is a sleuth hunting down mystery clues to solve a classroom crime or helping her mom unload forty loaves of bread from their weekly grocery store run, the delightful stories in *Bedtime Stories for the Child in You: A Memoir* will warm your heart. To learn more visit Louise's website: louisejewellonline.com

CPSIA information can be obtained
at www.ICGtesting.com
Printed in the USA
LVHW020342080423
743458LV00003B/3

9 781738 866908